contents

gourmet beef burgers

preparation time 15 minutes cooking time 10 minutes
serves 4

750g minced beef
1 cup (70g) stale breadcrumbs
2 tablespoons finely chopped fresh flat-leaf parsley
2 tablespoons sun-dried tomato paste
125g mozzarella cheese, sliced thinly
½ cup (150g) mayonnaise
4 bread rolls
50g mixed salad leaves
1 small red onion (100g), sliced thinly
2 tablespoons drained, sliced sun-dried tomatoes in oil

1 Combine beef, breadcrumbs, parsley and 1½ tablespoons of the paste in large bowl. Using hands, shape mixture into four burgers.
2 Cook burgers on heated oiled barbecue, uncovered, until browned and cooked through. Top burgers with cheese; cook until cheese melts.
3 Combine remaining paste and mayonnaise in small bowl.
4 Split rolls in half. Place cut-side down onto barbecue; cook until lightly toasted.
5 Sandwich burgers, mayonnaise mixture, salad leaves, onion and sliced tomatoes between bread rolls.

per serving 39.2g fat; 3219kJ (769 cal)

beef burgers with mustard mayonnaise

preparation time 20 minutes
cooking time 15 minutes
serves 4

500g minced beef
½ cup (40g) packaged stuffing mix
½ cup (60ml) tomato sauce
¼ cup coarsely chopped fresh
flat-leaf parsley
2 large white onions (400g),
sliced thinly
4 hamburger buns
8 oak leaf lettuce leaves
1 large tomato (250g), sliced thinly
1 tablespoon wholegrain mustard
½ cup (150g) mayonnaise

1 Combine beef, stuffing mix, sauce and parsley in medium bowl. Using hands, shape mixture into four burgers.
2 Cook burgers on heated oiled barbecue, uncovered, until browned and cooked through.
3 Meanwhile, cook onion on heated oiled barbecue plate until soft and browned.
4 Split hamburger buns in half. Place cut-side down onto barbecue; cook until lightly toasted.
5 Top base of buns with lettuce, tomato, patties, combined mustard and mayonnaise, then onion; replace top of buns.

per serving 26.6g fat; 2322kJ (555 cal)

mexican burgers

preparation time 20 minutes cooking time 10 minutes serves 6

750g minced beef
310g can red kidney beans, rinsed, drained
4 spring onions, chopped finely
2 fresh red thai chillies, deseeded, chopped finely
1 teaspoon hot paprika
1 tablespoon tomato paste
6 hamburger buns
6 round lettuce leaves
1 small avocado (200g), mashed
½ cup (120g) soured cream
2 tablespoons lemon juice

1 Combine beef, beans, onion, chilli, paprika and paste in medium bowl. Using hands, shape mixture into six patties.
2 Cook patties on heated oiled barbecue, uncovered, until well browned and cooked through.
3 Split buns in half. Place cut-side down onto barbecue; cook until lightly toasted.
4 Top base of buns with lettuce, patties and combined avocado, sour cream, and juice. Replace top of buns, if desired

per serving 26.9g fat; 2090kJ (499 cal)

cantonese beef burgers with grilled gai lan

preparation time 30 minutes **cooking time** 15 minutes **serves** 4

800g minced beef
1 medium brown onion (150g), chopped finely
3 cloves garlic, crushed
2cm piece fresh ginger (10g), grated
1 fresh small red thai chilli, chopped finely
227g can water chestnuts, drained, rinsed, chopped finely
¼ cup finely chopped fresh chives
1 egg
½ cup (35g) fresh breadcrumbs
1 tablespoon hoisin sauce
1 tablespoon water
2 tablespoons oyster sauce
⅓ cup (80ml) hoisin sauce, extra
2 teaspoons sesame oil
1kg gai lan (Chinese broccoli), chopped coarsely

1 Combine beef, onion, two-thirds of the garlic, ginger, chilli, chestnuts, chives, egg, breadcrumbs and hoisin sauce in large bowl; shape mixture into eight burgers.
2 Combine the water, oyster sauce, extra hoisin sauce and remaining garlic in small bowl. Reserve ¼ cup (60ml) hoisin mixture.
3 Brush burgers with remaining hoisin mixture; cook burgers, both sides, in heated oiled grill pan about 10 minutes or until cooked.
4 Heat sesame oil in same grill pan; cook gai lan until wilted. Serve gai lan topped with burgers, drizzled with reserved hoisin mixture.

per serving 20.2g fat; 2077kJ (497 cal)

lamb & bulgur wheat burgers

preparation time 25 minutes cooking time 20 minutes
serves 4

½ cup (80g) bulgur wheat
½ cup (125ml) boiling water
250g minced lamb
1 small brown onion (80g), chopped finely
1 small courgette (90g), grated coarsely
¼ cup finely chopped fresh mint
1 egg
1 tablespoon olive oil
4 bread rolls (660g)
½ baby cos lettuce, torn
1 large tomato (220g), sliced thinly
1 cup (240g) hummus

1 Place bulgur wheat in small bowl, cover with the boiling water; stand 10 minutes or until bulgur softens and water is absorbed.
2 Combine bulgur in medium bowl with lamb, onion, courgette, mint and egg. Shape mixture into four burgers.
3 Heat oil in large frying pan; cook burgers, over medium heat, until browned both sides and cooked through.
4 Meanwhile, preheat grill.
5 Split rolls in half; toast cut sides. Sandwich lettuce, burgers, tomato and hummus between roll halves.

per serving 28.3g fat; 3407kJ (815 cal)

lamb burgers with beetroot & tzatziki

preparation time 20 minutes **cooking time** 10 minutes
serves 4

500g minced lamb
1 small brown onion (80g), chopped finely
1 medium carrot (120g), grated coarsely
1 egg
2 tablespoons finely chopped fresh flat-leaf parsley
1 teaspoon finely grated lemon rind
½ teaspoon dried oregano leaves
2 cloves garlic, crushed
½ cup (140g) plain yogurt
½ cucumber (130g), deseeded, chopped finely
1 tablespoon finely chopped fresh mint
1 loaf ciabatta bread (430g)
1 cup (60g) coarsely shredded cos lettuce
225g can sliced beetroot, drained
1 lemon (140g), cut into wedges

1 Using hand, combine lamb, onion, carrot, egg, parsley, rind, oregano and half of the garlic in medium bowl; shape lamb mixture into four burgers. Cook on heated oiled grill plate (or grill or barbecue) until cooked as desired.
2 Meanwhile, combine yogurt, cucumber, mint and remaining garlic in small bowl. Cut bread into four pieces; split each piece in half horizontally. Toast bread cut-side up.
3 Sandwich lettuce, burgers, yogurt mixture and beetroot between bread pieces. Serve with lemon wedges.

per serving 19.3g fat; 2441kJ (584 cal)

lamb & feta burgers

preparation time 20 minutes   cooking time 10 minutes   serves 4

400g minced lamb
1 small (80g) brown onion, chopped finely
1 clove garlic, crushed
⅓ cup (40g) pitted black olives, chopped
60g low-fat feta cheese, crumbled
½ cup (35g) stale breadcrumbs
1 egg white

1 Combine all ingredients in bowl; mix well. Shape mixture into 8 burgers.
2 Heat oiled large pan; cook burgers until browned both sides and cooked through.

per serving 6.4g fat; 808kJ (193 cal)

lamb fritters with spicy yogurt

preparation time 10 minutes cooking time 20 minutes serves 4

2 teaspoons ground cumin
1 cup (280g) Greek-style yogurt
1 egg
1¾ cups (260g) self-raising flour
1½ cups (375ml) buttermilk
150g butternut squash, grated finely
2 spring onions, chopped finely
300g leftover roast lamb, chopped coarsely
vegetable oil, for shallow-frying

1 Dry-fry cumin in large frying pan, stirring, until fragrant.
2 Combine yogurt with half the cumin in small bowl.
3 Combine egg, flour and buttermilk in large bowl with squash, onion, lamb and remaining cumin; mix well.
4 Heat oil in same pan; shallow-fry quarter cups of batter, in batches, until fritters are browned lightly. Drain on absorbent paper; serve with yogurt.

per serving 49.2g fat; 3511kJ (840 cal)

lamb burgers with beetroot relish & yogurt

preparation time 30 minutes **cooking time** 45 minutes **serves** 4

500g minced lamb
1 small brown onion (80g), chopped finely
2 cloves garlic, crushed
1 teaspoon ground cumin
1 egg, beaten lightly
1 tablespoon olive oil
¾ cup (210g) greek-style yogurt
½ teaspoon ground cumin, extra
1 tablespoon finely chopped fresh mint
1 long loaf ciabatta
50g baby rocket leaves

beetroot relish
⅓ cup (80ml) water
4 medium beetroots (700g), trimmed, grated coarsely
1 small brown onion (80g), chopped finely
½ cup (110g) white sugar
⅔ cup (160ml) apple cider vinegar

1 Make beetroot relish.
2 Meanwhile, using hand, combine lamb, onion, garlic, cumin and egg in medium bowl; shape mixture into four burgers.
3 Heat oil in large frying pan; cook burgers, uncovered, until browned both sides and cooked as desired. Cover to keep warm.
4 Combine yogurt, extra cumin and mint in small bowl.
5 Cut ciabatta into quarters; halve quarters horizontally. Toast ciabatta pieces, cut-side up. Sandwich rocket, burgers, yogurt mixture and relish between ciabatta pieces.

beetroot relish Combine the water, beetroot and onion in large non-stick frying pan; cook, covered, about 15 minutes or until beetroot is tender. Stir in sugar and vinegar; cook, covered, stirring occasionally, 20 minutes. Uncover; cook, stirring occasionally, about 10 minutes or until liquid evaporates.

tip Beetroot relish will keep, covered and refrigerated, for up to three days.

per serving 22g fat; 3173kJ (759 cal)

lamb burgers with tomato salsa

preparation time 30 minutes (plus standing and refrigeration time)
cooking time 30 minutes **serves** 6

1 medium aubergine (300g)
coarse cooking salt
2 tablespoons olive oil
6 bread rolls
120g rocket
½ cup (40g) flaked parmesan

⅓ cup (50g) pitted black olives,
   chopped
¾ cup (50g) stale breadcrumbs
2 tablespoons finely chopped
   fresh basil
1 egg, beaten lightly

burgers
600g minced lamb
1 medium brown onion (150g),
   chopped finely
2 cloves garlic, crushed
⅓ cup (50g) drained, chopped
   sun-dried tomatoes in oil

tomato salsa
1 large red pepper (350g)
3 small tomatoes (390g), chopped finely
1 small red onion (100g), chopped finely
1 teaspoon balsamic vinegar
1 teaspoon finely chopped fresh
   oregano

1 Cut aubergine into 1.5cm slices; place in strainer. Sprinkle with salt; stand 30 minutes.

2 Rinse aubergine under cold running water; drain on absorbent paper. Brush aubergine with oil. Cook aubergine on heated oiled barbecue, uncovered, until browned both sides and tender.

3 Split rolls in half. Place cut-side down onto barbecue; cook until lightly toasted. Fill with aubergine, burgers, rocket, cheese and tomato salsa.

burgers Combine ingredients in medium bowl; mix well. Using hands, shape mixture into six burgers; place on tray. Cover; refrigerate 30 minutes. Cook on heated oiled barbecue, uncovered, until browned and cooked through.

tomato salsa Quarter pepper; remove seeds and membranes. Cook pepper on heated oiled barbecue, skin-side down, until skin blisters and blackens. Peel away skin, slice flesh thinly. Combine pepper with remaining ingredients.

per serving 22.4g fat; 2152kJ (514 cal)

pork chutney burgers

preparation time 20 minutes cooking time 10 minutes
serves 4

500g minced pork
1 cup (100g) packaged breadcrumbs
1 egg, beaten lightly
1 tablespoon finely chopped fresh flat-leaf parsley
2 tablespoons fruit chutney
2 tablespoons grated cheddar cheese
4 hamburger buns
2 lettuce leaves, shredded
1 medium tomato (190g), sliced thinly
4 canned pineapple rings

1 Combine pork, breadcrumbs, egg and parsley in medium bowl. Using hands, shape mixture into four burgers; flatten slightly. Indent centres; spoon combined chutney and cheese into centre of each burger. Shape burgers around chutney mixture to enclose mixture; flatten slightly.
2 Cook burgers on heated oiled barbecue, uncovered, until browned and cooked through.
3 Split buns in half. Place cut-side down onto barbecue; cook until lightly toasted.
4 Top base of buns with lettuce, tomato, pineapple and burgers; top with extra chutney, if desired. Replace top of buns.

per serving 14.6g fat; 2096kJ (501 cal)

chilli pork burgers

preparation time 15 minutes **cooking time** 20 minutes
serves 4

700g minced pork
1 small red onion (100g), chopped finely
⅓ cup coarsely chopped fresh coriander
¼ cup (15g) stale breadcrumbs
1 egg
1 fresh long red chilli, chopped finely
4 hamburger buns (360g)
⅓ cup (100g) mayonnaise
50g mizuna or rocket leaves
⅓ cup (25g) fried shallots

caramelised pepper salsa
1 medium red pepper (200g), sliced thinly
1 large red onion (300g), sliced thinly
½ cup (125ml) sweet chilli sauce

1 Combine pork in large bowl with onion, coriander,
breadcrumbs, egg and chilli; shape mixture into four burgers.
2 Cook burgers on heated oiled grill plate until cooked through.
3 Meanwhile, make caramelised pepper salsa.
4 Split buns in half; toast cut sides. Spread mayonnaise on bun
bases; sandwich mizuna, burgers, salsa and shallots between
bun halves.

caramelised pepper salsa Cook pepper and onion on heated
oiled flat plate until onion softens. Add sauce; cook, turning
gently, about 2 minutes or until mixture caramelises.

per serving 26.6g fat; 3018kJ (722 cal)

asian chicken burgers

preparation time 15 minutes cooking time 25 minutes serves 4

1 teaspoon groundnut oil
10cm stick (20g) finely chopped fresh lemongrass
1 small red onion (100g), chopped finely
½ teaspoon five-spice powder
½ teaspoon dried chilli flakes
1 tablespoon fish sauce
2 teaspoons finely grated lime rind
140ml can coconut cream
2 tablespoons crunchy peanut butter
500g minced chicken
1 cup (70g) stale breadcrumbs
¼ cup finely chopped fresh coriander
1 egg
1 medium carrot (120g)
½ cucumber (130g)
4 hamburger buns

1 Preheat grill.
2 Heat oil in small frying pan; cook lemongrass and onion, stirring, until onion softens. Add five-spice, chilli, sauce, rind and coconut cream; bring to a boil. Boil sauce mixture, uncovered, until reduced by half; cool 5 minutes.
3 Combine half of the sauce with peanut butter in small bowl. Combine remaining sauce with chicken, breadcrumbs, coriander and egg in large bowl; use hands to shape chicken mixture into four burgers.
4 Using vegetable peeler; slice carrot and cucumber into thin strips.
5 Cook burgers in heated lightly oiled large frying pan, uncovered, about 15 minutes or until cooked through.
6 Meanwhile, halve buns horizontally; toast, cut-sides up, under preheated grill. Spread peanut butter mixture on bun tops; sandwich burgers, carrot and cucumber between bun halves.

per serving 29.5g fat; 2746kJ (657 cal)

burgers italian-style

preparation time 20 minutes **cooking time** 30 minutes
serves 4

500g minced chicken
¼ cup (35g) sun-dried tomatoes, drained, chopped finely
1 tablespoon finely chopped fresh basil
1 egg
1 cup (70g) stale breadcrumbs
3 cloves garlic, crushed
4 slices pancetta (60g)
1 square loaf focaccia (440g)
½ cup (150g) mayonnaise
40g baby rocket leaves
120g mozzarella, sliced thickly

1 Combine minced chicken in large bowl with tomato, basil, egg, breadcrumbs and about a third of the garlic; shape mixture into four burgers.
2 Cook burgers on heated oiled grill plate about 30 minutes or until cooked.
3 Cook pancetta on grill plate until crisp. Drain.
4 Quarter focaccia; slice each square in half horizontally. Toast cut sides on grill plate.
5 Combine mayonnaise with remaining garlic, spread on focaccia bases; sandwich rocket, burgers, pancetta and cheese between focaccia quarters.

per serving 34.9g fat; 3357kJ (803 cal)

chicken burgers
with avocado cream

preparation time 30 minutes cooking time 10 minutes serves 4

800g minced chicken
2 rashers lean bacon (140g), chopped finely
⅓ cup (25g) grated parmesan cheese
3 spring onions, chopped finely
1 tablespoon finely chopped fresh thyme
1 egg, beaten lightly
½ cup (50g) packaged breadcrumbs
20cm square focaccia
1 cup (55g) mangetout sprouts
2 medium tomatoes (260g), sliced thinly
1 medium carrot (120g), sliced thinly

avocado cream
1 medium avocado (250g), chopped coarsely
125g cream cheese, softened
1 tablespoon lemon juice

1 Combine chicken, bacon, cheese, onion, thyme, egg and breadcrumbs in medium bowl. Using hands, shape mixture into four burgers.
2 Cook burgers on heated oiled barbecue, uncovered, until browned and cooked through.
3 Cut focaccia into four pieces; split each in half. Place cut-side down onto barbecue; cook until lightly toasted.
4 Top focaccia bases with sprouts, burgers, tomato, avocado cream and carrot.

avocado cream Combine ingredients in bowl; mash with a fork until well combined.

per serving 45.4g fat; 3473kJ (830 cal)

ginger, chicken & lime burgers

preparation time 10 minutes **cooking time** 20 minutes **serves** 4

340g chicken breast fillets
1 tablespoon grated lime rind
1 tablespoon grated fresh ginger
2 teaspoons ground cumin
1 egg white
2 spring onions, sliced
¼ cup (35g) plain flour

chilli sauce
2 medium (400g) red peppers
1 medium (150g) brown onion, chopped finely
4 birdseye chillies, chopped finely
415g can diced tomatoes
1 tablespoon brown sugar

1 Blend or process chicken until finely chopped. Add rind, ginger, cumin, egg and onion; process until mixture forms a paste.
2 Using hands, shape mixture into 8 burgers, coat in flour; shake away excess flour.
3 Heat oiled large pan; cook burgers about 2 minutes each side or until browned. Place burgers on oven tray, bake, uncovered, in moderate oven about 15 minutes or until cooked through. Serve with chilli sauce.

chilli sauce Quarter peppers, remove and discard seeds and membranes. Roast under grill or in very hot oven, skin-side up, until skin blisters and blackens. Cover pepper pieces in plastic or paper for 5 minutes, peel away skin, chop pieces finely. Heat oiled small pan; cook onion and chilli, stirring, about 2 minutes or until onion is soft. Stir in tomato and sugar, simmer, uncovered, 5 minutes; stir in pepper.

per serving 4.3g fat; 901kJ (215 cal)

salmon & green bean potato burgers

preparation time 20 minutes (plus refrigeration time)
cooking time 30 minutes serves 4

150g green beans
800g potatoes, chopped coarsely
20g butter
⅓ cup (25g) finely grated parmesan
1 egg
415g can red salmon
⅓ cup (35g) packaged breadcrumbs
vegetable oil, for shallow-frying
150g baby spinach leaves
1 medium lemon (140g), cut into wedges

1 Boil, steam or microwave beans until tender; drain. Rinse under cold water; drain. Chop coarsely.
2 Boil, steam or microwave potatoe until tender; drain. Mash potato in large bowl with butter, cheese and egg until smooth.
3 Drain salmon; discard skin and bones. Add salmon and beans to potato mixture; mix well. Shape salmon mixture into 12 burgers; coat in breadcrumbs. Place burgers on tray, cover; refrigerate 30 minutes.
4 Heat oil in large frying pan; shallow-fry burgers, in batches, until browned lightly and heated through. Drain on absorbent paper; serve on baby spinach with lemon wedges.

per serving 51.7g fat; 2959kJ (708 cal)

deep-fried salmon patties

preparation time 20 minutes (plus refrigeration time) cooking time 15 minutes
makes 8

5 small potatoes (480g)
440g can salmon
1 trimmed stick celery (75g), chopped finely
1 small white onion (80g), grated
1 small red pepper (150g), chopped finely
1 tablespoon finely chopped fresh flat-leaf parsley
1 teaspoon grated lemon rind
1 tablespoon lemon juice
½ cup (75g) plain flour, approximately
1 egg, beaten lightly
2 tablespoons milk
1 cup (100g) packaged breadcrumbs, approximately
1 cup (70g) stale breadcrumbs, approximately
vegetable oil, for deep frying

1 Boil, steam or microwave potatoes until tender; drain well. Place in medium
bowl; mash until smooth. Drain salmon well; remove skin and bones. Add to
bowl; mash using fork. Add celery, onion, pepper, parsley, rind and juice; mix
well using fork. Cover; refrigerate 30 minutes to make mixture easier to handle.
2 Divide salmon mixture evenly into eight portions; a simple way is to form
mixture into a round and divide into eight wedges. Shape each portion into patty;
dust with flour. Shake away excess flour; brush patties with combined egg and
milk. Toss in combined breadcrumbs; reshape if necessary while patting on the
breadcrumbs.
3 Place patties into frying basket, in batches. Lower gently into hot oil; deep-fry
about 2 minutes or until golden brown. Drain on absorbent paper. Serve with
lemon wedges, if desired.

tip Patties can be prepared a day ahead and refrigerated, covered.

per serving 28.6g fat; 1581kJ (378 cal)

thai fish burgers

preparation time 20 minutes cooking time 15 minutes serves 4

500g white fish fillets, chopped coarsely
1 tablespoon fish sauce
1 tablespoon kecap manis
1 clove garlic, quartered
1 fresh small red thai chilli, chopped coarsely
50g green beans, trimmed, chopped coarsely
¼ cup (20g) fried shallots
¼ cup coarsely chopped fresh coriander
60g baby spinach leaves
½ cucumber (130g), deseeded, sliced thinly
1 tablespoon lime juice
2 teaspoons brown sugar
2 teaspoons fish sauce, extra
4 hamburger buns (360g)
⅓ cup (80ml) sweet chilli sauce

1 Blend or process fish, sauce, kecap manis, garlic and chilli until smooth. Combine fish mixture in large bowl with beans, shallots and coriander; shape into four burgers.
2 Cook burgers on heated oiled flat plate about 15 minutes or until cooked.
3 Combine spinach, cucumber, juice, sugar and extra sauce in medium bowl.
4 Split buns in half; toast cut-sides. Sandwich salad, burgers and sweet chilli sauce between bun halves.

tip Any firm white fish fillets can be used in this recipe.

per serving 5.3g fat; 1722kJ (412 cal)

fish burgers

preparation time 15 minutes **cooking time** 20 minutes
serves 4

600g shark fillets, chopped coarsely
1 egg
¼ teaspoon sweet paprika
1 teaspoon ground cumin
1 teaspoon ground coriander
½ teaspoon garlic salt
40cm loaf ciabatta bread
1 cucumber (260g)
¾ cup (210g) natural yogurt
1 tablespoon finely chopped fresh mint

1 Blend or process fish, egg, paprika, cumin, coriander
and garlic salt until smooth. Using hands, shape mixture into
four burgers.
2 Cook burgers on heated oiled barbecue (or grill or grill plate),
uncovered, until browned and cooked through.
3 Cut bread into four pieces; split each in half. Place cut-side
down onto barbecue (or under grill); cook until lightly toasted.
4 Using a vegetable peeler, slice cucumbers into thin strips.
5 Combine remaining ingredients in small bowl.
6 Top bread bases with burgers; top with equal amounts of
cucumber and yogurt mixture, then remaining bread.

tip We used shark in this recipe; it has a sweet flavour with a
soft texture. Other white-fleshed fish can be substituted.

per serving 6.6g fat; 2193kJ (524 cal)

macadamia prawn burgers

preparation time 30 minutes **cooking time** 30 minutes serves 4

¾ cup (180ml) orange juice
¼ cup (60ml) lemon juice
2cm piece fresh ginger (10g),
   chopped coarsely
1 teaspoon black peppercorns
2 tablespoons white vinegar
½ cup (125ml) dry white wine
½ cup (75g) toasted macadamias
750g cooked peeled small prawns

1 egg, beaten lightly
1 tablespoon finely grated orange rind
4 spring onions, chopped finely
1½ cups (110g) stale breadcrumbs
1 long ciabatta loaf
2 tablespoons vegetable oil
4 egg yolks
250g butter, melted
80g watercress

1 Combine juices, ginger, peppercorns, vinegar and wine in small pan; bring to a boil. Reduce heat; simmer, uncovered, about 8 minutes or until citrus mixture reduces to ½ cup. Remove from heat; strain into small jug.

2 Meanwhile, blend or process nuts until finely chopped; place in large bowl. Blend or process 500g of the prawns until mixture forms a paste; place in bowl with nuts. Add remaining prawns, egg, rind, onion and 1 cup of the breadcrumbs; using hands, shape mixture into eight burgers. Press remaining breadcrumbs on to both sides of burgers; place on tray.

3 Cut bread into four pieces; split each piece in half horizontally. Toast, cut-side up, under hot grill until browned lightly; cover to keep warm.

4 Heat oil in large frying pan; cook burgers, in batches, until browned both sides and heated through. Cover to keep warm.

5 Meanwhile, blend or process egg yolks with citrus reduction until combined. With motor operating, add butter in thin, steady stream; process until sauce thickens.

6 Place two pieces of toast on each serving plate; top with watercress then two burgers and drizzle with sauce.

per serving 80.9g fat; 4943kJ (1181 cal)

tofu & vegie burger

preparation time 20 minutes (plus standing time) cooking time 20 minutes
(plus refrigeration time) serves 4

300g firm silken tofu
1 tablespoon olive oil
1 medium brown onion (150g), chopped finely
2 cloves garlic, crushed
¼ teaspoon sweet paprika
1 teaspoon ground turmeric
2 teaspoons ground coriander
1 small courgette (90g), grated coarsely
2 cups (140g) fresh breadcrumbs
¾ cup (190g) hummus
¼ cup (70g) greek-style yogurt
1 loaf ciabatta bread (430g)
⅓ cup coarsely chopped fresh mint
½ cup coarsely chopped fresh flat-leaf parsley
1 spring onion, sliced thinly
30g mangetout sprouts, trimmed

1 Pat tofu dry with absorbent paper. Spread tofu, in single layer, on absorbent-paper-lined tray; cover tofu with more paper, stand 20 minutes.
2 Meanwhile, heat oil in medium frying pan; cook brown onion and garlic, stirring, until onion softens. Add spices; cook, stirring, until fragrant.
3 Combine onion mixture in large bowl with tofu, courgette and breadcrumbs; shape into four burgers. Cover; refrigerate 30 minutes.
4 Meanwhile, combine hummus and yogurt in small bowl.
5 Cut bread into four pieces. Split each piece in half horizontally; toast cut sides in heated oiled grill pan.
6 Cook burgers in same oiled grill pan until browned both sides and hot.
7 Spread bread with hummus mixture; sandwich combined mint, parsley and spring onion, burgers and sprouts between bread pieces.

per serving 24.1g fat; 2880kJ (689 cal)

chilli & mint aubergine burgers

preparation time 20 minutes **cooking time** 10 minutes
serves 4

¼ cup (35g) plain flour
2 eggs
½ cup (85g) polenta
1 teaspoon hot paprika
1 medium aubergine (300g)
vegetable oil, for shallow-frying
1 large loaf ciabatta bread (430g), quartered
8 large round lettuce leaves
80g cheddar cheese, cut into 4 slices
½ cup loosely packed fresh mint leaves
⅓ cup (80ml) sweet chilli sauce

1 Place flour in small shallow bowl; beat eggs in second
small shallow bowl; combine polenta and paprika in third small
shallow bowl.
2 Slice aubergine into 8 slices crossways; discard two skin-side
pieces. Coat slices, one at a time, in flour, shake away excess,
dip in egg then coat in polenta mixture.
3 Heat oil in large frying pan; shallow-fry aubergine, in batches,
until browned lightly both sides. Drain on absorbent paper.
4 Meanwhile, preheat grill.
5 Halve each quarter of bread horizontally. Toast cut sides
under grill.
6 Sandwich lettuce, aubergine, cheese, mint and sauce
between toasted bread quarters.

per serving 23g fat; 2684kJ (642 cal)

sweet chilli beef ribs

preparation time 10 minutes (plus marinating time)
cooking time 30 minutes **serves** 4

½ cup (125ml) sweet chilli sauce
1 tablespoon soy sauce
¼ cup (60ml) rice wine
2 cloves garlic, crushed
1 teaspoon grated fresh ginger
2 tablespoons finely chopped fresh coriander
1.5kg beef spare ribs

1 Combine sauces, wine, garlic, ginger and coriander in large shallow dish; add ribs. Cover; refrigerate 3 hours or overnight.
2 Cook ribs in covered barbecue, using indirect heat, following manufacturer's instructions, about 30 minutes or until browned all over and cooked as desired.

per serving 11.4g fat; 1206kJ (288 cal)

beef spare ribs

preparation time 10 minutes (plus marinating time)
cooking time 20 minutes serves 4

2 cups (500ml) tomato sauce
½ cup (125ml) worcestershire sauce
¾ cup (180ml) vegetable oil
½ cup (125ml) water
¼ cup (60ml) white vinegar
⅓ cup (75g) firmly packed brown sugar
1 medium brown onion (150g), chopped finely
1.5kg beef spare ribs

1 Combine sauces, oil, the water, vinegar, sugar and onion in large shallow dish; add ribs. Cover; refrigerate 3 hours or overnight.
2 Drain ribs; reserve marinade.
3 Place reserved marinade in small saucepan; bring to a boil. Reduce heat; simmer, uncovered, until thickened slightly.
4 Cook ribs on heated oiled barbecue, uncovered, until browned and cooked through. Pour sauce over ribs. Serve with salad, if desired.

per serving 54.1g fat; 3999kJ (955 cal)

spicy veal rib cutlets

preparation time 5 minutes (plus marinating time)
cooking time 10 minutes serves 6

2 tablespoons oyster sauce
1 tablespoon fish sauce
1 tablespoon tamarind sauce
2 tablespoons groundnut oil
2 teaspoons ground cumin

2 teaspoons ground coriander
¼ teaspoon chilli powder
1 tablespoon sambal oelek
2 cloves garlic, crushed
6 veal rib cutlets (900g)

1 Combine sauces, oil, spices, sambal oelek and garlic in shallow dish; add veal. Cover; refrigerate 3 hours or overnight.
2 Cook cutlets on heated oiled barbecue, uncovered, until browned and cooked as desired.

per serving 9.3g fat; 841kJ (201 cal)

chinese barbecued spare ribs

preparation time 15 minutes (plus refrigeration time)
cooking time 1 hour **serves** 4

¾ cup (180ml) barbecue sauce
2 tablespoons dark soy sauce
1 tablespoon honey
¼ cup (60ml) orange juice
2 tablespoons brown sugar
1 clove garlic, crushed
2cm piece fresh ginger (10g), grated
2kg slabs american-style pork spare ribs

1 Combine sauces, honey, juice, sugar, garlic and ginger in large shallow dish; add ribs, turn to coat in marinade. Cover; refrigerate 3 hours or overnight.
2 Preheat oven to 180°C/160°C fan-assisted.
3 Brush ribs both sides with marinade; place, in single layer, in large shallow baking dish. Roast, covered, 45 minutes. Uncover; roast about 15 minutes or until ribs are browned. Serve with fried rice, if desired.

tip Ask your butcher to cut pork spareribs 'american-style' for this recipe. These will be slabs of 8 to 10 ribs, cut from the mid-loin, with almost all of the fat removed.

per serving 26.4g fat; 2675kJ (640 cal)

tex-mex ribs

preparation time 5 minutes (plus marinating time)
cooking time 45 minutes serves 4

1 cup (250ml) barbecue sauce
2 teaspoons chilli powder
2 x 35g packets taco seasoning
2kg american-style pork spare ribs

1 Combine sauce, chilli powder and seasoning in large shallow dish; add ribs. Cover; refrigerate 3 hours or overnight.
2 Place ribs in disposable baking dish. Cook in covered barbecue, using indirect heat, following manufacturer's instructions, about 45 minutes or until ribs are cooked through, brushing ribs occasionally with pan juices during cooking.

per serving 31.2g fat; 2455kJ (586 cal)

american-style pork spare ribs

preparation time 15 minutes (plus marinating time)
cooking time 10 minutes serves 8

1.5kg american-style pork spare ribs
1 cup (250ml) tomato juice
2 teaspoons grated lime rind
¼ cup (60ml) lime juice
2 tablespoons brown sugar
1 clove garlic, crushed
1 fresh red thai chilli, seeded, chopped finely

1 Cut rib racks into individual ribs.
2 Combine remaining ingredients in large bowl; add ribs. Cover; refrigerate 3 hours or overnight. Drain ribs; discard marinade.
3 Cook ribs on heated oiled barbecue, uncovered, until browned and cooked through.

per serving 16.8g fat; 1086kJ (259 cal)

honey mustard glazed ribs

preparation time 10 minutes (plus marinating time)
cooking time 45 minutes **serves** 4

½ cup (125ml) orange juice
½ cup (175g) honey
½ cup (125ml) barbecue sauce
2 tablespoons soy sauce
1 tablespoon wholgrain mustard
3 cloves garlic, crushed
2kg american-style pork spare ribs

1 Combine juice, honey, sauces, mustard and garlic in large shallow dish; add pork. Cover; refrigerate 3 hours or overnight.
2 Drain pork; reserve marinade.
3 Place ribs in disposable baking dish. Cook ribs in covered barbecue, using indirect heat, following manufacturer's instructions, about 45 minutes or until cooked through, brushing ribs occasionally with reserved marinade during cooking. Sprinkle with orange rind and coriander, if desired.

per serving 30.4g fat; 2705kJ (646 cal)

sticky pork ribs

preparation time 10 minutes (plus marinating time)
cooking time 45 minutes **serves** 4

2 tablespoons tomato paste
2 tablespoons tomato sauce
2 tablespoons soy sauce
1 teaspoon grated lemon rind
¼ cup (60ml) lemon juice
1 tablespoon brown sugar
1 teaspoon cracked black pepper
1 teaspoon ground allspice
¼ teaspoon chilli powder
2 cloves garlic, crushed
2kg american-style pork spare ribs

1 Combine paste, sauces, rind, juice, sugar, pepper, allspice, chilli powder and garlic in large shallow dish; add pork. Cover; refrigerate 3 hours or overnight.

2 Remove ribs from marinade; reserve marinade.

3 Place ribs in disposable baking dish. Cook ribs in covered barbecue, using indirect heat, following manufacturer's instructions, about 45 minutes or until ribs are cooked through, brushing ribs occasionally with reserved marinade during cooking.

per serving 30.4g fat; 1968kJ (470 cal)

barbecued spare ribs with red cabbage coleslaw

preparation time 15 minutes (plus refrigeration time)
cooking time 25 minutes serves 4

barbecue sauce

1 cup (250ml) tomato sauce
¾ cup (180ml) cider vinegar
2 tablespoons olive oil
¼ cup (60ml) worcestershire sauce
⅓ cup (75g) firmly packed brown sugar
2 tablespoons american mustard
1 teaspoon cracked black pepper
2 small red thai chillies, finely chopped
2 cloves garlic, crushed
2 tablespoons lemon juice

2kg slabs american-style pork
  spareribs

red cabbage coleslaw

½ cup (120g) soured cream
¼ cup (60ml) lemon juice
2 tablespoons water
½ small red cabbage (600g), shredded
  finely
3 spring onions, sliced thinly

1 Make barbecue sauce.
2 Place ribs in large shallow baking dish. Pour sauce over ribs, cover; refrigerate
3 hours or overnight, turning ribs occasionally.
3 Make red cabbage coleslaw.
4 Drain ribs; reserve sauce. Cook ribs on heated oiled grill plate, brushing
occasionally with reserved sauce, about 15 minutes or until cooked. Turn ribs
midway through cooking time.
5 Bring remaining sauce to a boil in small saucepan; cook about 4 minutes or
until sauce thickens slightly.
6 Cut ribs into serving-sized pieces; serve with hot sauce and coleslaw.

barbecue sauce Combine ingredients in medium saucepan; bring to a boil.
Cool 10 minutes.

red cabbage coleslaw Combine soured cream, juice and the water in
screw-top jar; shake well. Combine dressing in large bowl with cabbage and
onion. Cover; refrigerate until required.

per serving 39.9g fat; 3210kJ (768 cal)

chipotle pork ribs with chorizo & smoked paprika

preparation time 20 minutes cooking time 2 hours 50 minutes serves 4

4 chipotle chillies
1 cup (250ml) boiling water
1.5kg pork belly ribs
1 tablespoon olive oil
2 medium red onions (340g), chopped coarsely
1 medium red pepper (200g), chopped coarsely
1 medium green pepper (200g), chopped coarsely

1 chorizo (170g), sliced thinly
1 teaspoon smoked paprika
4 cloves garlic, crushed
3 x 400g cans crushed tomatoes
2 medium tomatoes (300g), chopped finely
½ cup finely chopped fresh coriander
2 teaspoons finely grated lime rind
1 clove garlic, crushed, extra

1 Preheat oven to moderately low.
2 Soak chillies in the boiling water in small heatproof bowl for 10 minutes. Discard stalks from chillies; reserve chillies and liquid.
3 Using heavy knife, separate ribs. Heat oil in large deep flameproof baking dish; cook ribs, in batches, until browned all over.
4 Cook onion, peppers, chorizo, paprika and garlic in same dish, stirring, until onion softens. Return ribs to dish with undrained crushed tomatoes, chillies and reserved liquid. Cover; cook in moderately low oven about 1 hour.
5 Uncover; cook in moderately low oven about 1½ hours or until ribs are tender.
6 Meanwhile, combine chopped tomato, coriander, rind and extra garlic in small bowl. Cover; refrigerate until required.
7 Top ribs with coriander mixture; serve with roasted corn salsa and flour tortillas, if desired.

roasted corn salsa Roast 3 husked corn cobs on heated oiled grill plate (or grill) until browned all over. When cool cut kernels from cobs and combine with 1 chopped small red onion, 1 chopped medium avocado, 250g halved cherry tomatoes, 2 tablespoons lime juice and ¼ cup chopped fresh coriander.

per serving (incl. salsa) 97.7g fat; 5300kJ (cal 1268)

texan-style spare ribs

preparation time 20 minutes (plus refrigeration time)
cooking time 2 hours 5 minutes **serves** 8

3kg american-style pork spare ribs
2 tablespoons sweet paprika
1 tablespoon ground cumin
1 teaspoon cayenne pepper
2 x 800ml bottles beer
1 cup (250ml) barbecue sauce
¼ cup (60ml) water
¼ cup (60ml) maple syrup
¼ cup (60ml) cider vinegar

1 Place ribs on large tray. Combine spices in small bowl, rub spice mixture all over ribs. Cover; refrigerate 3 hours or overnight.
2 Preheat oven to moderate (180°C/160°C fan-assisted).
3 Bring beer to a boil in medium saucepan. Reduce heat; simmer, uncovered, 20 minutes. Divide beer and ribs between two large shallow baking dishes;
cook, covered, 1½ hours. Remove from oven; discard beer.
4 Meanwhile, combine sauce, the water, syrup and vinegar in small saucepan; bring to a boil. Reduce heat; simmer, uncovered, 5 minutes.
5 Cook ribs, in batches, on heated barbecue (or grill or grill plate), turning and brushing with sauce occasionally, until browned all over.

per serving 17.5g fat; 2123kJ (cal 508)

glossary

allspice also known as pimento or jamaican pepper; available whole or ground.

american-style pork spare ribs trimmed, long mid-loin pork ribs; sold in racks of eight or 10 ribs.

barbecue sauce a spicy, tomato-based sauce used to marinate, baste or as an accompaniment.

breadcrumbs

packaged fine-textured, crunchy, purchased, white breadcrumbs.

stale 1- or 2-day-old bread made into crumbs by grating or processing.

bulgur wheat also known as burghul; hulled steamed wheat kernels that, once dried, are crushed into various size grains.

buttermilk fresh low-fat milk cultured to give a slightly sour taste; low-fat yogurt or milk can be substituted.

cheese

cream commonly known as 'Philadelphia', a soft milk cheese having no less than 33% butterfat.

feta a crumbly goat or sheep's milk cheese with a sharp salty taste.

mozzarella a semi-soft cheese with a delicate, fresh taste and a stringy texture when hot.

parmesan an aged, sharp-tasting, dry, hard cheese, made from skimmed or part-skimmed milk.

chillies come in many types and sizes, fresh and dried. Wear rubber gloves when handling, as chillies can burn your skin. Removing seeds and membranes lessens the heat.

chipotle a dried, smoked jalapeño chilli with a deep, intense, smokey flavour. Dark brown in colour, they are available in cans.

flakes crushed dried chillies.

thai small, medium hot, and bright-red to dark-green in colour.

chorizo a Spanish sausage made of coarsely ground pork and highly seasoned with garlic and chillies.

ciabatta popular Italian crisp-crusted white bread.

coconut cream obtained from the first pressing of the coconut flesh, without the addition of water. Available in cans and cartons.

cumin available both ground and as whole seeds; cumin has a warm, earthy, rather strong flavour.

fish sauce made from pulverised salted fermented fish, mostly anchovies. Has a pungent smell and strong taste; use sparingly.

five-spice powder a fragrant mixture of ground cinnamon, cloves, star anise, sichuan pepper and fennel seeds.

foccacia a flat Italian-style bread.

gai lan also known as chinese broccoli; leaves and stem are used.

ginger also known as green or root ginger; the thick gnarled root of a tropical plant.

groundnut oil oil pressed from ground peanuts; most commonly used in Asian cooking because of its high smoke point.

hoisin sauce a thick, sweet, spicy Chinese paste made from fermented soy beans, onions and garlic.

hummus dip made from chickpeas, garlic, lemon juice and tahini (sesame seed paste).

kecap manis an Indonesian sweet, thick soy sauce which has sugar and spices added.

lemongrass a tall, lemon-smelling and tasting, sharp edged grass; use only the white lower part of the stem.

maple syrup a thin syrup distilled from the sap of the maple tree. Maple-flavoured syrup is not an adequate substitute.

mustard

american flavoured with sugar and vinegar or white wine; is bright yellow and very mild in flavour.

wholegrain A French-style coarse-grain mustard made from crushed mustard seeds and Dijon-style French mustard.

oyster sauce a rich brown sauce made from oysters and soy sauce.

pancetta Italian unsmoked cured pork belly; bacon can be substituted.

paprika ground dried red pepper; available sweet, hot or smoked.

polenta also known as cornmeal; a flour-like cereal made of dried, ground corn (maize).

sambal oelek a salty paste made from ground chillies.

sesame oil made from roasted, crushed, white sesame seeds; for flavouring rather than cooking.

shallots, fried available in jars or cellophane bags from Asian grocery stores. You can make your own by frying thinly sliced peeled shallots until golden-brown and crisp.

soy sauce made from fermented soy beans; several varieties are available.

sweet chilli sauce mild, Thai sauce made from red chillies, sugar, garlic and vinegar.

taco seasoning a packaged seasoning mix of oregano, cumin, chillies and various other spices.

tamarind sauce if unavailable, soak about 30g dried tamarind in a cup of hot water. Stand 10 minutes and squeeze pulp as dry as possible; use the flavoured water.

tofu (bean curd) made from the 'milk' of crushed soy beans; comes fresh as soft or firm. Silken tofu refers to the method of straining the soy liquid through silk.

vinegar

balsamic made from an Italian wine of white trebbiano grapes aged in antique wooden casks to give the exquisite pungent flavour.

rice wine made from rice wine lees (sediment), salt and alcohol.

water chestnuts small brown tubers with a crisp, white, nutty-tasting flesh. Best fresh, however, canned are more easily obtained.

worcestershire sauce a thin, dark-brown spicy sauce.

conversion charts

MEASURES

The cup and spoon measurements used in this book are metric: one measuring cup holds approximately 250ml; one metric tablespoon holds 20ml; one metric teaspoon holds 5ml.

All cup and spoon measurements are level.

The most accurate way of measuring dry ingredients is to weigh them. When measuring liquids, use a clear glass or plastic jug with metric markings.

We use large eggs with an average weight of 60g.

warning This book may contain recipes for dishes made with raw or lightly cooked eggs. These should be avoided by vulnerable people such as pregnant and nursing mothers, invalids, the elderly, babies and young children.

DRY MEASURES

METRIC	IMPERIAL
15g	½oz
30g	1oz
60g	2oz
90g	3oz
125g	4oz (¼lb)
155g	5oz
185g	6oz
220g	7oz
250g	8oz (½lb)
280g	9oz
315g	10oz
345g	11oz
375g	12oz (¾lb)
410g	13oz
440g	14oz
470g	15oz
500g	16oz (1lb)
750g	24oz (1½lb)
1kg	32oz (2lb)

LIQUID MEASURES

METRIC	IMPERIAL
30ml	1 fl oz
60ml	2 fl oz
100ml	3 fl oz
125ml	4 fl oz
150ml	5 fl oz (¼ pint/1 gill)
190ml	6 fl oz
250ml	8 fl oz
300ml	10 fl oz (½ pint)
500ml	16 fl oz
600ml	20 fl oz (1 pint)
1000ml (1 litre)	1¾ pints

LENGTH MEASURES

METRIC	IMPERIAL
3mm	⅛in
6mm	¼in
1cm	½in
2cm	¾in
2.5cm	1in
5cm	2in
6cm	2½in
8cm	3in
10cm	4in
13cm	5in
15cm	6in
18cm	7in
20cm	8in
23cm	9in
25cm	10in
28cm	11in
30cm	12in (1ft)

OVEN TEMPERATURES

These oven temperatures are only a guide for conventional ovens.
For fan-assisted ovens, check the manufacturer's manual.

	°C (CELSIUS)	°F (FAHRENHEIT)	GAS MARK
Very low	120	250	½
Low	150	275–300	1–2
Moderately low	160	325	3
Moderate	180	350–375	4–5
Moderately hot	200	400	6
Hot	220	425–450	7–8
Very hot	240	475	9

index